BETWEEN PERSON AND PLACE

Conservation Histories From The Kennebec Land Trust

INTERVIEWS BY: KATIE EPSTEIN

EDITED BY: THERESA KERCHNER, BARBARA LIBBY, AND DEBORAH SEWALL

KENNEBEC LAND TRUST

Editorial team: Katie Epstein, Theresa Kerchner,
Barbara Libby and Deborah Sewall

Layout and Design: LPK

Map, page 48: Center for Community GIS, Farmington, Maine

Subjects: Conservation, History, Kennebec Land Trust,
Land Trusts, Maine, Oral History, Philanthropy

ISBN 978-1-4507-2000-7

Epstein, K., Kerchner, T., Libby, B., and Sewall, D. 2010.
Between Person and Place: Conservation Histories from the Kennebec
Land Trust. Kennebec Land Trust, Winthrop, Maine.

For

The Kennebec Land Trust's past and
future land donors, volunteer stewards,
and especially, Mort and Barbara Libby

Acknowledgements

The Kennebec Land Trust appreciates
the contributions of our land donors
and photographers; Katie Epstein; the
Maine conservationists who provided
insightful quotes; Deborah Sewall;
Emily Perkins; and LPK's talented staff in
Cincinnati, Ohio (Rick Conner, Creative
Director; Michelle Cromer, Brand Leader;
Jeff Winkle, Senior Designer; Paula Egbers,
Implementation Specialist)

BETWEEN PERSON AND PLACE

When I first started this project, I thought that in many ways I knew Kennebec County and the small town of Wayne where my family spent so many summers. As I approached the interview process with my own host of memories and special places, I was eager to learn more about the forests and lakesides I had explored. I envisioned an iconic Maine landscape preserved for public enjoyment.

Many of the properties featured within this book are just that — beautiful and idyllic places that have been conserved for public recreation and appreciation. But when we know the stories of the people who donated these properties, a piece of land becomes more than a place to walk, seek quiet, or enjoy wildlife. We have a deeper understanding of those who called each place home. Some properties are working landscapes and were preserved to maintain an agrarian economy. Some are living memorials, places of education and history where visitors can physically walk through the past. Others are recreation sites or wildlife habitats for some of Maine's most charismatic critters.

The reasons for donation were equally diverse, and sometimes complicated. Families conserved land in honor of loved ones, to improve the community, or to preserve a valuable piece of land in perpetuity. My hope is that in reading these narratives you will hear the voices of the people who donated each wonderful property.

Every donor I spoke with was hopeful for the future of Maine and for rural communities. Their stories illuminate the inextricable connection between person and place.

— Katie Epstein, KLT Intern

Contents

INTRODUCTION

Every place has a story. *Between Person and Place: Conservation Histories from the Kennebec Land Trust*, is one chapter in a complex story about the relationships between land and people in Kennebec County, Maine.

In 2009, with twenty years of work behind us and eighteen land donors available for interviews, we set out to learn more about our own conservation history. Katie Epstein, our summer intern from Davidson College, framed a set of questions and worked throughout the summer to write essays based on the interviews she recorded.

If you own land, roam the countryside, or spend summers in Maine, you likely have something in common with the people Katie interviewed. Maybe, above all, you value seasonal changes — familiar plants that bloom in spring or summer, wildlife that arrive to breed on a predictable time schedule. If you are or were a farmer, the sight and smell of newly mown hay might bring back memories of hard, hot work and well-earned independence. If you are a summer resident, watching sunrise over a clear lake or hiking on a well-worn path might be just what you yearn for all year long.

Kennebec County is a mosaic of forested hills, villages and small cities, ponds and lakes, agricultural fields, and biologically rich wetlands. At first glance, it may seem that there are only small variations between one forested ridgeline and the next, and from pond to pond. Katie's writing focuses and sharpens our views of KLT's ecological and public commons. Through the lens of these stories, we are able to see and appreciate land and place.

— *Theresa Kerchner, Executive Director*

Life ran back and forth, land into people and people back into land, until both were the same.

— Lura Beam, *A Maine Hamlet*

Elizabeth Davidson and Deb Sewall at Davidson Nature Preserve *(©Kennebec Journal/Joe Phelan)*

BEARNSTOW PARKER POND
CONSERVATION EASEMENT, MT. VERNON

LAND DONOR: RUTH GRAUERT

Bearnstow, Parker Pond (*Richard Bird*)

To make the long trip to Maine from Hartford, Connecticut, Ruth Grauert had to save up several months' worth of gasoline coupons. It was 1945, a difficult time in the United States. "There was racial prejudice, religious prejudice, economic prejudice… it just wasn't a very open society." Eager to create change, Ruth wanted to use her experience working as a dancer to start a children's summer camp.

She was looking for a specific setting. It had to be remote, beautiful, and untamed — enough to give children a wilderness experience. The camp was going to be a place for kids from all backgrounds. After considering many properties throughout central Maine, Ruth settled on 74 acres on the remote shores of Parker Pond in Mount Vernon. No one had lived on the property since 1938. Ruth laughs as she recalls walking the long driveway and climbing over seven years of fallen limbs. "We looked in this building first, and it was full of liquor bottles," says Ruth, who thinks fishermen used it for shelter in the winter. "It was a mess, but later we went to the ledges and looked out over the pond. It was so quiet. Then I knew; this had to be the place."

The camp's name, Bearnstow, means "children's place" in Early West Saxon. True to its name, it is a mystical landscape of towering hemlocks, flowering groundcover, cedar swamps, and narrow birch-lined footpaths. Over the years, Bearnstow has become a refuge for children of all ages. Now the camp offers weeklong dance workshops for teens and adults in addition to the day camp for children. Workshops attract dancers of all abilities as well as enthusiasts who come for both the world class instruction and the extraordinary setting.

Ruth encourages using Bearnstow's landscape as a source of creative inspiration. "We've had people dance on the camp porches, in the creek, and slide down the rock cascade into the pond. A trio of young women once did an underwater ballet in the deep water around the dock where we stood to watch, probably one of the more beautiful pieces produced at Bearnstow. I don't recall the name of the choreographer nor the performers, but their work is memorable."

Children make the most of their surroundings by canoeing, hiking forest

Ruth Grauert
(Jane Davis: 2009)

trails, and digging clay out of the banks of the small creek that runs through the property. "A part of every day is spent in nature study." The children learn the names of local plants and to step carefully around the trilliums and lady slippers. They eat wild blueberries and Indian cucumber root. Returning campers take responsibility for passing on these lessons. "They really learn to respect the earth."

To assure the camp buildings would stay rustic and the land undeveloped, Ruth developed a conservation easement for the entire Bearnstow property with the Kennebec Land Trust. "It has to remain as it is," she says.

Ruth hopes to conserve several other pieces of personal property. "Easements are wonderful tools for preserving the land." Ruth plans to run the camp as long as she can. "It's not lucrative and it doesn't always pay the bills, but it does good work and that's what life's about."

Besides being a whole lot of fun, summer camps help kids and adults develop confidence, self-reliance, and a sense of stewardship for the outdoors.

— Scott Olsen,
Bryant Pond 4-H Camp,
Bryant Pond, Maine

Bearnstow *(Richard Bird)*

Ladyslipper
(Lauren Bushner Silva)

CURTIS HOMESTEAD
CONSERVATION AREA

LAND DONORS: KEN CURTIS AND REBECCA CURTIS MEREDITH
OWNED BY: KLT, LEEDS

Curtis Oak Island *(Jane Davis)*

Like much of the landscape surrounding it, KLT's Curtis Homestead Conservation Area has been in constant transition. Today, even-aged pine, mixed-aged hardwood, and mature hemlock stands dominate where there were once hayfields, pastures, orchards, and a woodlot. Three miles of trails meander through the property, crossing stone walls that are vivid reminders of Maine's 19th century era of subsistence and diversified farming.

Part of a wave of English emigration, William and Deborah Curtis moved to Maine from Tenterden, England, in the early 1800's. In 1817, they purchased land along a stream in the small town of Leeds and began clearing the land for a farm. Their farmhouse and barn, built in the 1840's, became the center of Curtis life and activity for the next 150 years, and remained standing until the 1990's.

Thin topsoil and a short growing season made farming in rural Maine a hardscrabble life, and it was no different for the Curtis family. Kenneth Curtis, who grew up on the property during its last years as a working farm, describes his childhood neighbors as hard-working and independent. Ken's father Archie "wouldn't have done anything else if he could have." To make ends meet, they raised a few dairy and beef cows and some chickens, and grew corn and beans to sell to local canneries. Ken recalls, "Virtually nothing was wasted."

During the long winters, Ken helped his father selectively log the north end of their land. This provided their yearly firewood as well as supplementary income. The wood was pulled out by horses, along a narrow logging road that forms one of the walking trails on the property today.

To escape from chores, Ken and his sister, Rebecca, spent summer afternoons exploring, picking highbush blueberries, and fishing in the small stream that runs through the property. Kenneth remembers that some of the best brook trout could be found near an old beaver dam. "The beavers made a hole and the fish liked to get into the deeper water. You could drop a line right by the beaver house and catch good size trout."

Today, walking trails follow the edge of the brook and bog where Ken and Rebecca trekked. From Curtis Rock, a large glacial erratic where Ken remembers he'd stop to catch his

Ken Curtis
(Jym St. Pierre)

breath, visitors can take in a view of the bog* that surrounds an upland island with impressive red oaks.

Ken's parents, Archie and Harriet Curtis, continued farming until the 1960's. Looking toward the future, Ken and Rebecca wanted to honor their family's history on the property. "When we thought about how hard people had worked on the farm, the best thing we could do was leave the land in their memory." In 2000, Ken and Rebecca donated all 360 acres to the Kennebec Land Trust for permanent conservation and public use.

The landscape of the Curtis Homestead continues to evolve. Each year as forest growth reclaims more of the former farmland, its agrarian imprint fades. Visitors to the property now find a glimpse of Maine settlement history, and diverse habitats that benefit both wildlife and local residents. One local high school, Monmouth Academy, holds outdoor ecology classes here.

Elementary school students are learning about forest succession patterns on abandoned farmland, and the value of locally based sustainable forest management, logging, and lumber production. Ken Curtis and Rebecca Curtis Meredith have left a Maine legacy for generations to come.

*Ecologists in Maine would classify the Curtis "bog" as it is locally known, as a fen. Fens develop due to the influence of mineralized ground and surface waters such as the stream that flows into the area. The area is thus high in nutrients where as true bogs are nutrient poor and more acidic than fens.

Brook trout
(Duane Raver, USFWS)

Maine is the last bastion of wild brook trout in the United States. Their presence is a true indicator of high water quality.

— Steve Brooke,
Maine State Council,
Trout Unlimited

Curtis farmhouse *(Ken Curtis: 1942)*

DAVIDSON
NATURE PRESERVE

LAND DONOR: ELIZABETH DAVIDSON
OWNED BY: KLT, VASSALBORO

Davidson Nature Preserve (Brian Kent)

Regardless of the season, you can count on Elizabeth Davidson to have a freezer stocked with blueberries from the fields next door, part of the Davidson Nature Preserve, 97 acres that she donated to the Kennebec Land Trust in 2005. Since her donation, many Vassalboro neighbors have written to thank her, sharing fond memories of grandparents spending classic Maine summer days picking blueberries in these fields.

Elizabeth was raised near Boston and spent childhood summers in South China, Maine. Afterwards, she went west to teach in the Music Department at the University of California, Berkeley. Elizabeth says, "I missed New England dearly, especially the fall, the seasons, and family." She retired in 1990, came back to the east coast, and made Vassalboro home with her purchase of land that is now the Davidson Nature Preserve.

With her new land came the question of whether to continue mowing the blueberry fields. "At first I thought — I can't afford to have them mowed season after season — I'll let them grow wild. But a neighboring farmer told me that when one thinks of the work that went into clearing these fields, and that farmers only used oxen, and then built these impressive stone walls… well that did it. I realized the open fields were cultural icons." The fields are now mowed on a rotating basis, which ensures the preserve's much-loved annual blueberry crop.

While the mowing question took some thought, Elizabeth knew from the start that she wanted to preserve the property. In a town that was rapidly losing open space and farmland, she understood that land conservation should be a priority. Before partnering with the KLT, Elizabeth contacted several organizations whose headquarters were out of the state, but decided that when protecting lands of local significance, "You may not want someone from away." Working with the Kennebec Land Trust would ensure that her land would be cared for by "an organization that knew and cared about land and people in my community."

Visitors to the Davidson Nature Preserve come for more than blueberries. They can also observe a variety of natural habitats. A white pine-mixed hardwood forest surrounds the expansive blueberry fields, providing diversity and edges for both forest and meadow species. At the western end of the field is a wetland — a long fen, like a bog, but with nutrient input from a flowing stream. When beaver impounded the stream and flooded the surrounding upland, the fen became home to a great blue heron rookery, which currently supports nineteen impressive stick nests. Preserve visitors marvel at the view of the rookery, with nests high in the limbs of dead trees, and the activity of herons during the spring and summer breeding and foraging seasons.

The Preserve's conservation land is enhanced by the neighbor's abutting woodlot and orchard. Elizabeth notes, "Any contiguous land that provides habitat for wildlife is a great advantage." She feels fortunate to have been able to protect and share a diverse, well-loved property. "I know it is something that a lot of people would like to do; finding a group who immediately understood my goals made this possible."

Heron rookery (©Kennebec Journal/Joe Phelan)

The Davidson Nature Preserve is home to a portion of one of Maine's largest inland great blue heron colonies. Protection from human development and habitat alteration undoubtedly facilitated its formation and growth, and will likely allow it to persist for several decades.

— Danielle E. D'Auria, Wildlife Biologist, Bird Group Maine Department of Inland Fisheries & Wildlife

Elizabeth Davidson
(Sarah Fuller)

Lowbush blueberry, *Vaccinium angustifolium*
(Maine Natural Areas Program)

FLYING POND FARM
CONSERVATION EASEMENT, VIENNA

LAND DONORS: ELLEN MILLER AND FAMILY

Flying Pond Farm
(Jym St. Pierre)

The five Miller siblings — Peter, Lynette, Holly, Rosemary and Robin — spent their early childhood in a northern New Jersey suburb. Their father commuted to the International Paper offices in New York. Both parents, Ellen and Robert Miller, were from upstate New York and wanted to get back to the country. In 1965, Robert transferred to the Androscoggin Mill in Jay, Maine, and purchased a 40-acre dairy, Flying Pond Farm, in Vienna.

Holly remembers, "The barn was in really good shape. I was thrilled about the move; I was going to be able to have a horse!"

The Millers were not farmers, but they had their fields hayed every year to keep them from becoming overgrown. They and their neighbors enjoyed an unobstructed view of the pond. The children wore paths through the fields to a favorite swimming spot and enjoyed skiing and snowshoeing the property in winter. Robin and Rosemary, who lived away from home, returned to the farm for vacations. Although Robert was "definitely interested in the farming," continues Holly, he never used the property for commercial production.

Ellen kept a large garden and planted trees around the farmhouse. Peter* carried firewood to keep the stoves running and remembered, "That was a big job, and nobody was overly warm."

"Dad loved that he could drive to work and never pass a car," Holly adds. "Coming from a suburban neighborhood, that was pretty special."

Ellen remained at Flying Pond after Robert passed away in 1978. She was concerned about potential commercial development on Route 41. Another concern was that the shores of Flying Pond itself had come under increasing development pressure during the Millers' time in Vienna. Though the pond frontage consists mainly of wetlands and is not suitable for development, it harbors abundant wildlife. The farm's fields slope away from the road to Flying Pond and Graves Brook, which flows into the pond. Loons nest in the marsh there, and the small, secluded cove at the mouth of Graves Brook is known locally as a prime fishing spot. Aware that none of her children planned to stay on the farm, Ellen saw a conservation easement as a way of preserving the natural beauty of the land, as well as a gift to the town of Vienna, her adopted home.

After Ellen Miller's death in 2001, Holly and Lynette continued the process of negotiating a conservation easement. Holly recalls, "First there was the idea of a conservation easement, but we also

The Miller children, left to right: Holly, Rosemary, Peter, Robin and Lynette
(Brenda Pinkham)

wanted to encourage farming." Working with KLT volunteer attorneys Howard Lake and Jeff Pidot, they crafted the trust's first easement for agriculture and open space.

The Millers were aware that an easement would make it more difficult to sell the property. Holly researched online and listed Flying Pond with the fledgling Maine Farm Link program. Its database helps retiring Maine farmers find new owners who will keep their property in agriculture. The goal is "to curb the conversion of Maine's farmland and to maintain the state's agricultural heritage for generations to come." This goal dovetailed with those of the Millers. "Within two days, Maine Farm Link received a phone call from a family in Pennsylvania who would eventually farm it organically," Holly says. "It was the first link that the program made."

The property has since been resold to a new family of organic farmers. They sell milk, eggs, and vegetables. Under the terms of the 2003 KLT agricultural easement, the owners may farm on the

40 acres, which are otherwise protected from development. The easement allows additions to or certain modifications of the existing farm home and outbuildings, so long as they are on the original farmstead.

The Miller family remains grateful to the KLT for making it possible to carry out Ellen Miller's desire to protect the place she loved. They were able to ensure that Flying Pond Farm will remain in agricultural use and offer beautiful views forever.

Reflecting on how they all loved their time on the farm, Robin notes that "we didn't really own the property, we were just lucky enough to live there. We're here for a short time. The land is there forever."

Peter Miller passed away in autumn of 2009, shortly after the interview for this book.

(Jane Davis)

Protecting farmland has so many benefits in addition to allowing continued crop production. The land may be used for recreation, to protect bodies of water, to support wildlife, and much more.

— Jean English, Editor, *The Maine Organic Farmer & Gardener*, Columnist, *Growing Points*

GOTT PASTURE
PRESERVE

LAND DONORS: GEORGE E. LADD III,
LINCOLN F. LADD, AND ROBERT M. LADD
OWNED BY: KLT, WAYNE

Gott Pasture
(Jym St. Pierre)

George Ladd first came to Wayne with his father in the early 1920's. They stayed at the Maurita Inn on Main Street, hired a horse and wagon, and asked the locals for the best place to fish. The Ladds were directed to Wilson Pond, where they spent several days fishing under an oak tree. George's son, Lincoln, recalls his father telling him that bass leapt out of the water straight onto their lines!

Inspired by the quiet beauty of Wilson Pond and their incredible fishing luck, George and his father inquired about the property. Land owner Luther Norris was willing to sell the undeveloped forested parcel, Lincoln says. "The land was for sale for back taxes, and my grandfather and father bought it jointly." That was in 1924. A small shuttered cabin and several tent platforms were built — and Camp Ladd began.

As predictably as the seasons, the Ladd family returns to Wilson Pond each summer. The original tent platforms have been replaced by a constellation of cabins along the shoreline. From June to September, more than one hundred members of the Ladd family make their way to Wayne, Maine from across the country. The culminating weekend is always July 4th when almost fifty Ladds reunite for fireworks and festivities. Family activities are typical of most Maine summer retreats. "The kids go canoeing and swimming. Everyone gathers in the camp's mess hall for

dinner, and cookouts are held on Saturday nights," says Robert, Lincoln's brother. Wildlife, including raucous herons in a nearby white pine rookery, have adapted to the visitors who have called this land a summer home for eighty years.

When their parents passed away, Lincoln, Robert, and their brother, George, decided to protect part of their family lands permanently. So, in 2003, they donated the 75 acres that George Ladd and his wife Helen had purchased in 1957 to the Kennebec Land Trust. This property, adjacent to the family camp, had been known locally as Gott Pasture, and Lincoln and Robert remember watching Charlie Gott's cows back when it was still a wooded pasture.

The Ladds, as well as visitors from surrounding communities, now frequent KLT's Gott Pasture throughout the summer. A wooden sign, parking area, and registration box welcome hikers, and a path follows the steep glacial ravines and shoreline. Visitors can stop to see a 19th-century farmstead foundation, impressive red oaks and white pines, and a vernal pool.

Robert Ladd knows what this land means to his family. "When you ask my kids where their roots are, they'll say Wayne." With the donation of Gott Pasture Preserve, visitors for generations to come will have the opportunity to develop their own connections to this permanently protected conservation land.

Wilson Pond, Gott Pasture *(Jym St. Pierre)*

Left to right: Robert Ladd, Lincoln Ladd, George Ladd *(Contributed)*

April rains and thawing temperatures herald one of the Northeast's most spectacular, if largely unnoticed, wildlife migrations. Emerging from the forest floor, legions of Maine's wood frogs and mole salamanders move en masse toward small woodland pools marking one of the first signs that spring has finally arrived.

— Phillip deMaynadier, Wildlife Biologist, Maine Department of Inland Fisheries and Wildlife

Wood frog *(Megan Gahl)*

HODGDON ISLAND
PRESERVE

LAND DONORS: ELLIOTT AND ANNE FARR
OWNED BY: KLT, WINTHROP

Cobbosseecontee Lake
(Mort Libby)

One of Martha Kent's favorite family photos is of her grandmother Katharine Elliott Farr (circa 1904) paddling a canoe solo on Lake Cobbosseecontee. "She had this beautiful red canoe," remembers Martha, "and she was always out in it. She and my grandfather loved to take long canoe trips."

Martha has boxes of photos of her family extending back several generations summering at Belle Island on Lake Cobbossee. "We're very lucky that my grandfather was an avid family historian and photographer and loved to make albums," says Martha.

Martha's family has owned land on or near Cobbossee since at least the early 19th century. "My great-great-grandfather, Moses Briggs, was a farmer and blacksmith, and he owned a mainland farm that stretched down to the Cobbossee shore. In the mid-19th century, he acquired several of the Cobbossee islands, including Belle Island and parts of Hodgdon's and Horseshoe."

Moses Briggs used the islands as woodlots for his farm and forge, and in the summer, the south-facing granite ledges of Belle Island were used for picnicking. In the late 19th century, summer cottages were built on Belle. The surrounding islands were left undeveloped for the most part, although some of the island interiors continued to be logged through the 1920's or '30's.

Over the years, Moses Briggs' many descendants have loved these islands and frequented them for a quiet paddle, some fishing, or a chance wildlife sighting. "As a child and teenager I often canoed in and around the small coves and passages of Hodgdon's and Horseshoe Islands looking for loons and other wildlife," Martha recalls. "There were these little enclosed places and you just felt like you were away from everything. Today, the lake is healthier than it was in the 1960's, and when we go out for a paddle we often see beaver, mink, muskrat, loons, osprey, heron, and bald eagles, among many others."

Martha notes how memories of Hodgdon's and Horseshoe became woven into family folklore. "My father, Elliott Farr, used to talk about this enormous 'virgin' pine on Horseshoe and he would take us to visit it when we were kids. I don't know if it's actually virgin, but it's really big! [In the Horseshoe cove] there's a big rock ledge. I'm told that my grandfather... proposed to my grandmother in a canoe right there."

Martha Kent
(Jane Davis)

Katharine Elliott Farr in canoe *(Contributed: circa 1904)*

When Elliott Farr inherited the island properties from his father, Clifford Bailey Farr, and from his mother's cousin, Loutrel Briggs, preservation was a family priority. "Loutrel and our grandfather thought that Elliott would do whatever he could to preserve the islands in their unspoiled state, and he was fully in agreement with that."

Martha's husband, Don, notes that before there was an organized land trust in Kennebec County, "The only way to preserve land was just to own it and pay the taxes. So when the Kennebec Land Trust came into being, my father-in-law jumped on it."

Elliott Farr spent time in his later life working to make sure the islands were conserved. Just after he passed away in 1995, 17 acres on Hodgdon's Island were officially opened as public conservation land. A trail now follows the island's perimeter, giving visitors access to dense cedar stands, an interior forest with massive red oaks and white pines, and stunning views of the island's wetlands and shoreline.

Part of Horseshoe Island passed to Martha's mother, Anne, after her father died. Martha remembers, "She also wanted it conserved." In 2004, Anne realized her wish and added an additional 3.5 acres to KLT's Horseshoe Island Conservation Area.

Today Elliott and Anne Farr's grandchildren, as well as local and summer residents, visit the same places generations before them did, and according to Martha, the family "couldn't be happier with the work that the Kennebec Land Trust has done and continues to do."

Meanwhile, Katharine had acquired a canoe, given her on her twenty-first birthday by her brother, which I named "Medawisla"(Loon), a name which I found in Thoreau's Maine Woods.

— Clifford B. Farr, Family Historian
and father of F. W. Elliott Farr

19

HORSESHOE ISLAND
PRESERVE

LAND DONOR: JON LUND
OWNED BY: KLT, WINTHROP

Horseshoe Island Preserve
(Jym St. Pierre)

Jon Lund is a sportsman. He loves hunting and fishing, especially in the remote woods of northern Maine. Jon is also a conservationist who spent his career in government working to conserve Maine's natural resources. Although these two roles are often perceived as conflicting, Jon has spent the better part of his life demonstrating that sportsmen and conservationists have common interests. He says, "All too often they end up on opposite sides, and I think that's not an accurate portrayal of their real interests."

In the mid-1930's, Jon's family moved to Augusta where his father reopened a paper mill that had been shut down during the Depression. Growing up, Jon learned about "the importance of jobs" and the connection between industry and natural resources.

He carried many of these lessons with him when he served as State Representative and Senator in the Maine State Legislature from 1965 to 1972. One of Jon's first controversial decisions was on a bill to lower water quality standards for Prestile Stream in order to accommodate the development of a sugar beet factory. Jon voted against the bill, while many of his contemporaries supported it. The business later collapsed, and investors and the State lost money. He says, "Having served as Kennebec County Attorney, my initial interest had been in criminal law. However, after the Prestile Stream case, I found a significant interest in conservation."

While serving as State Attorney General, Jon worked to demonstrate the economic and social benefits of renewable natural resources. "I grew into it as issues came along. I thought they were important to Maine. I can fully understand that we need jobs. The place where I disagree is when they say we either have to have jobs or a good natural resource base in Maine. It's not an either-or situation. I think you can conserve natural resources and still have industry."

His family had a camp on Hodgdon's Island on Lake Cobbosseecontee, where Jon spent summers fishing, sailing, and canoeing. Remembering Horseshoe Island in particular, Jon saw the value in preserving as much of it as possible, and set out to acquire property on the island.

His chance came when he joined the National Resources Council of Maine, where he met Cobbossee Lake summer resident Dorothea A. Marston. Dorothea

Jon Lund *(Jym St. Pierre)*

Jon Lund is the kind of hunter-naturalist-conservationist every sportsman and –woman should aspire to be: keenly aware that all creaturely life, human life included, depends on healthy habitat and that any civilization worthy of the name must protect the wild world from which it has sprung.

— Robert Kimber, Author

remembered canoeing and camping on Horseshoe Island as a young girl and shared Jon's interest in preserving it.

They made a plan. Dorothea owned a partial interest in property on Horseshoe. She sold her share to Jon. "Then I had to chase down the other owners." After lengthy correspondence, Jon managed to secure title to a piece of Horseshoe Island. He held on to the property until the late 1990's, when he learned about the Kennebec Land Trust. "I was in agreement with the goals and processes that KLT was following and I had a lot of confidence in the people who were active in it." In 1997, he donated 7 acres on the northeast arm of Horseshoe Island to the Kennebec Land Trust.

For Jon, donating the property put his government experience into action. Now retired, he focused his attention on public access. "What good is a conserved area if no one can visit it?" In order to increase public access

on Hodgdon Island Preserve, which was donated to KLT in 1994, Jon and his brothers volunteered to lay out a walking path there. "It's one of the few places in the area where you can walk for an hour and not hear traffic." With this one successful island trail completed in 2009, Jon and his brothers have proposed a second project — the KLT Horseshoe Island path — one more bridge between interests of the community and the environment.

Jon Lund and Mort Libby *(Theresa Kerchner)*

21

MACDONALD
CONSERVATION AREA

LAND DONORS: JESSIE AND DOUGLAS MACDONALD

OWNED BY: KLT, READFIELD

Macdonald woods *(Jym St. Pierre)*

In 1965, Douglas Macdonald needed a change. An author and English teacher, he was living In New York City. "I was tired of New York, tired of the crowds." Douglas hit the road and drove to Maine. "I wanted to start a farm. I had no experience, and I'm not sure where I got the dream." He was drawn to the "rawness" of living up north. "I just liked the idea of Maine," he says.

Douglas stopped in the town of Wayne. "I was impressed right away with the area and thought it was particularly beautiful." He met a landowner who was willing to sell him 100 acres of woodland and fields on the Readfield town line. The property had no house, only an old foundation. Needing somewhere to live, Douglas also purchased a small camp on Lake Androscoggin.

Several decades and a career change later, he and his wife, Jessie, now summer at the Androscoggin camp. "I never really got around to farming," Douglas admits. "I just let it go wild." He studied horticulture and became a landscape designer. "I realized that nature has the best design." Since farming was no longer part of their plans, Douglas and Jessie decided to keep the property as woodland.

In 2002, the Kennebec Land Trust approached the Macdonalds about conserving their property. Since the Macdonalds' land was adjacent to a town forest, there was added benefit to conserving two large wooded parcels. "I thought the idea of preserving forestland was a very good one," recalls Douglas.

On a walk with KLT staff and board members, the Macdonalds gained new appreciation for their property. "They pointed out all these wonderful plants" recalls Jessie. "And we just thought, 'Wow!'"

In 2004, Jessie and Douglas Macdonald donated their hundred acres to the Kennebec Land Trust. Several years later, KLT volunteers developed a path that connects to the Readfield Town Forest trails and features wooded views of Jones Brook. A registration box with maps and brochures now welcomes hikers to the trail. "We were not really using the land, and to open it up to the public in some way was a great thing. Just preserving land isn't enough," says Douglas. "You have to have people walk through it and enjoy it in some way."

The Macdonald Conservation Area joins the Readfield Town Forest to create a 210-acre conservation area.

Jessie and Douglas Macdonald
(Stan Macdonald: 2009)

The two areas contain several loop trails. In turn, these parcels are part of a much larger undeveloped forest that is habitat for a variety of species with extensive home ranges, like black bear, moose, and goshawk.

The Macdonalds try to walk the trails every time they visit. Donating their land helped them forge a deeper connection with an area they love and appreciate. Jessie says, "We've always cared what happens to the town, but now we feel really connected."

Bears are all about food. Their lives revolve around the search for and consumption of various foods that change with the seasons. It's forested habitat that provides that food and lots of it. Since bears eat a wide variety of foods, they require large tracts of undeveloped land with diverse habitat types included.

— Randy Cross, Bear Biologist, Maine Department of Inland Fisheries and Wildlife

Female black bear
(Tom Sears)

Mathews Wildlife Habitat
Fayette

LAND DONORS: ALICE POLLIS,
JANE BROGAN, AND STEPHANIE MATHEWS
OWNED BY: KLT, FAYETTE

Mathews
(Jym St. Pierre)

The Underwood Homestead in Fayette, built two centuries ago, remains a place of great beauty and peace. The Mathews family, who donated the property to the Kennebec Land Trust, also has deep roots in Fayette: they gather each summer at the camp built by Richard Mathews' grandfather in 1932.

Every summer Bette and Richard Mathews drove with daughters Alice, Jane, and Stephanie, from their home in Augusta to their camp. They always passed the farm that was part of the original Underwood Homestead, bordered by Echo Lake, Lovejoy Stream, and Lovejoy Pond. Stephanie remembers that her mother "fell in love with the property."

Joseph Underwood settled in Fayette in 1812 and became the town's first merchant. He was active in public affairs, representing Fayette in the General Court of Massachusetts and later in the Maine Legislature. The farmstead, crafted with care, still stands on the main road through town. According to the *History of Fayette,* the bricks were burned on the farm, and Mr. Underwood examined each one. To enclose the fields for his renowned herd of Hereford cattle, he constructed a system of stone walls; today they remain so straight and tidy that they appear new.

Eager to move to the country, Bette and Richard purchased 40 acres of the original Underwood property in 1960. According to Alice, the property "was all grassy and open, with fields full of cows, and you could see the impressive stone walls." They built a house on a high point to take advantage of the sweeping views. Richard spent many hours on his John Deere tractor maintaining the fields. "He loved to be out there mowing."

Bette and Richard had a strong spiritual connection to nature. The daughters recall their mother's rejoicing at the woodcocks' sound and the wood ducks' reappearance each spring. "She loved to sit on the porch, watching thunderstorms move in over Echo Lake, and the deer, woodchucks, foxes, and birds that frequented the fields around the house." Every season held wonders, and both Bette and Richard instilled in their daughters a great appreciation for the sounds, smells, and colors that filled their daily lives.

Visitors today can still hear loon calls echoing from the pond and the whoosh of blue herons taking flight from Lovejoy Stream. The boulder near the entrance

Bette and Richard Mathews
(Contributed)

contains an iron ring to which Mr. Underwood tethered his ox, while he stacked rocks into perfectly engineered stone fences. During the summer, the fields are full of wild strawberries, yarrow, cinquefoil, buttercups, black-eyed Susans, Queen Anne's lace, Indian paintbrush, juniper, mint, and daisies. (Richard kept the fields mowed, but always maneuvered around the daisies.)

The 200-year-old sugar maple — a magnificent tree of great girth and height in the southwest corner of the main field — was a magical place for youngest daughter Stephanie. Richard constructed a tree house for her high in its limbs. When he realized she was afraid to navigate the ladder, Richard built a grand staircase for his daughter. "When I reached the top, I would lie down on the platform and stare up through the gracious branches, like arms to the sky. It was as if you could touch heaven," Stephanie recalls.

Beneath this tree the family built a simple bench as a memorial to Richard and Bette. The couple had expressed two wishes for eternal peace. One was to have a resting place beneath the old maple, and the other was that the rolling fields and majestic stands of pine and hardwoods would remain home for birds, wildlife, flowers, and plants.

Richard predeceased Bette by six years. Before she passed away in 1997, she and her daughters discussed the future of the property. It was at this time that Jane learned about the Kennebec Land Trust. Several months later, the three daughters donated 17 acres to the KLT in memory of their parents.

The sisters are thrilled that KLT has joined the history of devoted owners of this part of the Underwood Homestead, ensuring future visitors the opportunity to explore and appreciate land that still holds a special place in their hearts.

Wildflowers *(Sarah Fuller)*

KLT properties contain many of Maine's plant species. These conserved lands give families the opportunity to learn about Maine's flora together, and are excellent outdoor classrooms for children.

— Eric Doucette, Botanist

25

The trail on KLT's 100-acre Parker Pond Headland parcel features 5,000 feet of rocky shoreline, an old-growth hemlock stand, and impressive granite ledges. Each year, hundreds of hikers visit this woodland preserve and hike a path that showcases the property's rich, complex, geologic, and human history.

PARKER POND
HEADLAND PRESERVE

LAND DONORS: ERIKA KARP AND TONY DILLER,
HODGKINS ADDITION TO PPH PRESERVE
DONATED BY: GLENN AND SARA HODGKINS
OWNED BY: KLT, FAYETTE

Parker Pond shoreline (Sarah Fuller)

An abrupt transition between young hardwood and mature hemlock marks the boundary between the 100-acre Parker Pond Headland and the 42-acre Hodgkins Addition to the Headland. The two parcels, with their very distinct forest stands, are important habitat for many of Maine's familiar plant and wildlife species.

Regarding Parker Pond, Tony Diller says, "My sister Erika and I inherited the land from our parents, Van and Berta, in 1989. They had bought it in two different transactions. The first, from Central Maine Power in 1954, included the northernmost tip of the headland, with the wonderful ledges where many have enjoyed picnics and swims. The second transfer was a land swap: the Parker Lake Shores developer agreed to trade some of Van and Berta's lakefront on Fellow's Cove in return for all of the "backlot." The backlot included the cliffs, old-growth hemlocks and the steep, rocky slope opposite Birch Island."

For the Hodgkins family, a serendipitous online search led them to the 42 acres

in Fayette that became the Hodgkins Addition to Parker Pond Headland. After visiting the property, Glenn and Sara Hodgkins knew the rolling hills and dense hardwood forest were more than just an ideal family summer camp. It was perfect property for a community land trust. Donating land to the Kennebec Land Trust had been on the Hodgkins' agenda for several years, and Glenn in particular saw the donation as an important part of his work as a land conservationist.

"Conservation has always been very important to me; it's the most important volunteer activity that I do." With twelve years on the KLT board, and two years as president, Glenn is dedicated to the KLT cause. He believes that a childhood outdoors in southern Maine was the root of his interest in conservation. "Maine is a special place that I value." His work as a hydrologist, studying Maine's waterways, has only reinforced his commitment to be proactive in public land work.

Tony Diller's experience on Parker Pond was similar. "When Erika and I

Glenn, Sara, Anna, and
Ben Hodgkins *(Contributed)*

were kids, we spent many hours hiking and exploring this area, swimming off the rocks, and learning about the different sorts of trees and plants. We had some great picnics, especially on the 4th of July. Even the loons joined in. Helen Cushman, a local naturalist, was often in the woods with us and would introduce us to which mushrooms we could eat and which ones were poisonous. When I was a bit older I used to camp out on top of the cliffs, sleeping in the 'bear cave.' Fortunately the bears left me alone."

Asked about their donation, Tony says, "Anyone on the lake can see immediately that the Parker foreshore is a very prominent part of the lake. Our parents realized the importance of preserving this land in as natural a condition as possible. Erika and I share their sentiments and have done what we think Van and Berta intended. We could see that making an agreement with the KLT would preserve the land in its natural state and the whole lake community would benefit, into the future."

Preserving Maine's forests is also a top priority for Glenn, whose goal is "to conserve what are currently the common woodlands, because eventually they won't be so common."

Glenn and Sara Hodgkins are, in many ways, unique donors to the Kennebec Land Trust. Although they don't have childhood memories of playing on the Hodgkins Addition trails, or a family legacy there to preserve, they share the same commitment to Maine's natural landscapes as the people who were committed to preserving the northern part of the Parker Headland.

The Headlands Preserve on Parker Pond is one of central Maine's hidden gems. The Land for Maine's Future Board had an easy decision to support this project.

— Tim Glidden, Director,
   Land for Maine's Future Program.

Artist Ian Ormon at Parker Pond
(Jane Davis: 2008)

Swimming at Loon Island, left to right: Chig Dollof, Erika Diller, Helen Cushman (famous local newspaper woman and story teller), friend Judy Adams, David Kirk, Cush (Norm) Cushman, Van Diller, Clayt Dollof *(Contributed, circa 1955)*

PERKINS WOODS

LAND DONORS: JOHN AND PAT PERKINS
OWNED BY: KLT, WAYNE

Perkins Woods shoreline
(Jane Davis)

John and Pat Perkins have spent almost 30 summers in a small green cabin nestled among tall pines and hemlocks. Sitting on their screened porch, the view is 180 degrees of quiet Androscoggin lakeshore. "It has everything we could ever want," explains Pat. "We just love it up here. We've only missed one year, and that was for the birth of our grandson."

John and Pat, now both retired, spend the majority of their time in Maine enjoying the outdoors and introducing their grandchildren to Maine's wildlife. Avid birders, they take great joy in the diversity of birdlife along their shoreline property and, like many local residents, are enthusiastic collectors of loon paraphernalia. They keep diligent watch over the neighborhood loon family. Pat created a homemade loon raft of cedar and styrofoam which the loons return to every year. "They seem to like it," says John.

The Perkins' camp is part of a larger shoreline development that was started by John's father, Jack, in the 1930's. John's Aunt Margaret purchased the property for her two nephews and their families after the rest of the cabins had been sold.

In 1980, John inherited the last remaining parcel of his father's development project, a 14-acre, old-growth forested peninsula abutting Camp Androscoggin, a summer camp for boys. Although it has no road access, the land does have 2,700 feet of wooded, rocky shoreline. Initially John and Pat were unsure what to make of the landlocked parcel.

Over the years, many shoreline developments on the lake have altered wildlife habitat. Nevertheless, John and Pat weighed development proposals and an offer from Camp Androscoggin Boys Camp. After much thought, John and Pat decided that these options did not make sense for them, their family, or their passions. Remembering how "nice it is to see undeveloped land adjacent to their developed neighborhood," they donated the 14-acre forested parcel to the Kennebec Land Trust in 2001 to ensure that it would remain a wooded preserve.

Paddling in by canoe or skiing across frozen Androscoggin Lake is the only way to access the short loop trail that circumnavigates the Perkins Woods. The property has fewer visitors than most KLT properties, but John and Pat

Pat and John Perkins
(Daniel Perkins)

are happy knowing the land will stay undeveloped, especially since the discovery of nesting ospreys. Visitors who make the journey across the lake to Perkins Woods are greeted by an impressive cathedral of 150-year-old white pines, eastern hemlocks, and red oaks.

The old growth offers a glimpse of what the Androscoggin shoreline must have looked like before summer camps and housing developments. John hopes the property will be enjoyed by their grandchildren and fellow residents. He and Pat know they made the right decision. John adds, with a wink in his eye, "It doesn't reduce my taxes that much, but all in all it was a worthwhile thing to do."

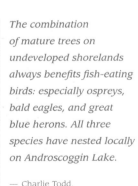

Osprey *(Elsa Martz)*

The combination of mature trees on undeveloped shorelands always benefits fish-eating birds: especially ospreys, bald eagles, and great blue herons. All three species have nested locally on Androscoggin Lake.

— Charlie Todd,
    Wildlife Biologist, Maine
    Department of Inland
    Fisheries and Wildlife

Red maple leaves
(Jane Davis)

THE WALTER A. AND ALICE B. REYNOLDS FOREST

SIDNEY

LAND DONOR: BEATRICE REYNOLDS

OWNED BY: KLT, SIDNEY

Reynolds Forest stream
(Emily Perkins)

In front of a house in Sidney, Maine sits an old iron washtub. The tub is a reminder of Beatrice Reynolds' childhood. Beatrice can remember sitting in it with her sister, the two of them pouring water over their heads with a tin pail at bath time. She has other heirlooms too, and family photos turned sepia with age decorate walls in her house.

Beatrice's interest in family and heritage is seen in her contributions to the community. She's donated time and artifacts to the Maine State Museum, and added to the Sidney historical archives. In 2004, Beatrice took her commitment to preservation a step further by donating 35 acres of her family's land to the Kennebec Land Trust. She named the forest after her parents to honor their lives in Maine. "I wanted it to be a memorial to them."

The Walter A. and Alice B. Reynolds Forest was part of 250 acres purchased by Beatrice's ancestor, John Marsh, in 1753. John, from Massachusetts, was one of the first Kennebec River settlers in Sidney. More than two centuries and seven generations later, Beatrice lives on part of the same 250-acre parcel and keeps up with the family history. When she was a child exploring her grandparents' attic, "I found an old Bible. I asked my father if I could have it and he said of course. I looked inside and I found the handwritten will of John Marsh." It was an exciting day for Beatrice, who later found the only existing birth records of several other family members.

The heart of Reynolds Forest is Marsh Brook. Bea notes that seven generations back, her ancestor John Marsh chose this land and kept it in family ownership because of the value of the brook for water power. "He knew how important that stream would be to the future generations who lived here." John harnessed the waterpower with a saw and grist mill, the foundations of which are still visible from trails within the forest.

Hikers have an authentic opportunity to learn about the use of natural resources by Maine's early settlers on the first public conservation land in Sidney. In addition to its historical ties, the property provides other popular features. The loop trail is a favorite of birding clubs. A hiking path leads to stone-lined, deep pools that provide beautiful picnic spots. And the conservation property has been a field research site for a Colby College

Glenn Hodgkins
and Bea Reynolds
(Nancy Ross)

student studying invasive plant
control methods.

Beatrice hopes that the Kennebec
Land Trust will use her family's land
to teach about local history and the
natural world. The dam structures
and geological features make this
conservation property a fascinating
outdoor classroom for students of all
ages. Visitors can climb up on the ridge,
look out at the land, and try to answer
the question, "How did it get this way?"

Kali Abel, KLT Intern, Colby College and Kents Hill Students *(Theresa Kerchner)*

Bea and her sister Alice, feeding hens in Sidney *(Contributed, 1942)*

*There is no better way for students to learn about the rich
natural beauty and historical significance of Reynolds Forest
than to experience it first-hand.*

--- Phil Downes, Teacher

SMALL-BURNHAM CONSERVATION AREA
LITCHFIELD

LAND DONORS: INA SMALL,
DUSTY SMALL, AND TEAGUE MORRIS

American Bittern
(Phil Downes)

Birdfeeders of all shapes and sizes dot the yard surrounding Ina Small's farmhouse. Dusty Small, Ina's stepson, jokes, "None of the neighbors ever see any birds, because they're always at Ina's." An avid birder, Ina hosts local bird clubs for walks around the property. The farm is a diverse landscape of pasture, woodland, and wetland. Although there is excellent birding throughout the 250 acres, it is hard to get the enthusiasts off the front porch.

Dusty's great-great-grandfather purchased the farm, which was then only 40 acres, in 1846. The property has remained in the family ever since. When Dusty's father, Granville Small, inherited the land in the mid-1950's, he set about assembling a larger farm out of neighboring tracts of land, including one previously owned by Dusty's mother's family, the Burnhams. "He wanted to make a better farm out of it," says Dusty. Granville added several large fields for hay and pasture. "We grew vegetables, and had sugar maples for syrup." Father and son tapped and collected all the sap for syrup by hand. "That's why my arms are so long," laughs Dusty. "I was carrying all those heavy buckets."

When Granville wasn't working on his farm, he was pursuing what Dusty calls his "real life work." Behind the farm were enormous gravel pits, dug mostly for the construction of the nearby interstate and state turnpike. "They were big ugly holes in the ground. My

father spent his whole life trying to fix these gravel pits. He used an irrigation system to wash out the cliffs and then spent hours on the tractor smoothing it down."

The gravel pits have been replaced with sloping fields and clear ponds with wooded edges. Today's naturalized landscape is a living tribute to Granville's passion. When he passed away in 2008, Ina, Dusty, and Dusty's partner, Teague Morris, were touched by the community response. "Many people remembered all he had done to restore this land. His passing really got us thinking," recalls Teague. In order to continue Granville's work, the three purchased another small gravel pit formerly owned by Dusty's grandfather and are in the process of restoring it. Knowing that Granville wouldn't want the farm developed, they also began weighing options for its future.

"We got a dog, and the dog gave us a good reason to get out and start walking around. The more you walk,

Teague Morris, Delmar Small, and Ina Small
(Jane Davis: 2009)

Swallows *(Jane Davis)*

the more you appreciate." Dusty adds, "I started looking at maps and saw that our property was connected to other properties in Litchfield that were semi-public. The fairgrounds, the big cemetery, the church, and the ball fields, we were all connected."

Ina, Dusty, and Teague have signed a conservation easement on approximately 250 acres. Their vision for Litchfield includes a town-wide trail system, an idea which is gathering support with their neighbors. The family is developing trails, cleaning up farm remnants, and continuing Granville's reclamation work. Dusty has submitted a plan to the Litchfield Conservation Commission to reclaim some pits on the far side of town.

Teague explains further, "The decision to place our property in conservation didn't come easily. Some of our friends wonder why we'd give up the right to develop the land and make a lot of money. To be sure, we're not rich people, but we love this land too much

to let that happen. What was harder to give up was the sense of privacy (control, really) and share what is so deeply, personally 'ours' with others. After a lot of soul searching, realizing we'd never be able to take care of all of this land forever, the best way to ensure its future is by sharing it with people who will look after it long after we're gone."

Designing an easement takes a long time, but according to Dusty, "My father proved that if you just keep at it for long enough, you can really do something."

> *Restored gravel pits are in an elite class of exemplary Maine wetlands. But don't take my word for it. Visitors should instead listen to the voices of bitterns, rails, marsh wrens, and waterfowl who raise families here.*
>
> — Ron Joseph, Wildlife Biologist, US Fish and Wildlife Service

Aerial view of gravel pits *(Glenn Parker)*

STURTEVANT FARM SCENIC AREA
CONSERVATION EASEMENT, FAYETTE

LAND DONORS: ARN AND LEDA STURTEVANT

(Jym St. Pierre)

Baldwin Hill Road in Fayette, Maine, climbs a forested ridge past the Fayette Baptist Church to Home-Nest Farm. On the eastern side of the road sits an old white farmhouse. The porch wraps to the front, the rocking chairs face west. The view is idyllic, 17 acres of open pasture, orchards, and stone walls, capped with a 60-mile panorama of the northern Appalachians.

Home-Nest Farm, owned by Arn and Leda Sturtevant, was built in 1784 and has been inhabited by nine successive generations of Sturtevants, including Arn and Leda's children, grandchildren, and great grandchildren. "My great-great-great grandfather, Andrew, was a soldier in the continental army," says Arn. "After his military service, he and his two brothers married three Besse sisters and settled in Wayne, Readfield, and Fayette. Andrew and his offspring cleared the Fayette land and expanded Home-Nest to accommodate a growing family." As a result of additions over the years, the rambling farmhouse is now a mix of architectural styles — Federal, Greek Revival, and Victorian.

Until the late 19th century, Home-Nest Farm was a subsistence farm. Many of Arn's ancestors were "lured away by the industrial revolution" after the Civil War. The homestead was temporarily unoccupied in the mid-20th century. In the 1970's, Arn and Leda inherited the farm. The former pastures were overgrown, and the couple remembers,

"We started clearing little by little until we got the view back."

They knew how important that view had been to previous generations. Arn and Leda, who can list their colonial ancestors the way most people recite the alphabet, have written a four-book series on family history called *Home-Nest Chronicles*. In *Josiah Volunteered*, Arn quotes a letter from his great-grandmother to her husband, who was fighting in the Civil War. "How many times we two had watched the sun go down behind those far western hills in all its glory," Helen Ormsby Sturtevant wrote. The vista has always been an integral part of life on the farm.

Arn and Leda placed a conservation easement on the property with the Kennebec Land Trust in 2003. "We didn't know what might happen years down the road," says Arn.

Today Home-Nest Farm is a country inn, with a small bench beside the road to welcome visitors. In the old farmhouse or in one of two cottages, guests enjoy a rare glimpse of 18th and 19th century

Arn and Leda
Sturtevant
(Jane Davis: 2009)

Maine farming. The Sturtevants think the vista is what makes the inn a place for inspiration and rest. According to Arn, the best site "is down along the blueberry fields on the crest of the pasture between the house and church, where we contemplate the double joy of picking the highbush berries and gazing on that inspiring westward view. We have visitors who return year after year."

Arn and Leda call the majestic sweep of the panorama a refreshing, soul-liberating influence. Knowing it is preserved brings them great satisfaction. Their easement is KLT's first property conserved for scenic value. For the Sturtevants, the easement preserves family history. For the community, it is, and will remain, simply a beautiful place.

(Jym St. Pierre)

The Sturtevants got their view back: the old pastures, the orchard, the hills, and mountains beyond — the view that Arn's great-grandmother reminded her husband of in her letter to him when he was away fighting in the Civil War. Imagine him, far from what he loved, carrying this vision like an amulet.

--- Susan Shetterly, Author

Helen Sturtevant and daughter May
(Contributed, 1863)

35

TYLER CONSERVATION AREA
CONSERVATION EASEMENT, READFIELD

LAND DONORS: JOHN W. AND MARJORIE TYLER

Tyler Woods *(Jym St. Pierre)*

When John and Marjorie Tyler replaced the floor in their farm house a few years ago, they found a half cent dated 1835 under three layers of old floor. It was in mint condition. Using that coin, they were able to estimate that their house was built in the early 1800's. John's parents, John Sr. and Mary Tyler, loved the solitude of the house when they purchased it in 1956. They bought the house and 60 acres for $3,600. They then spent the next 15 years renovating it.

John chose his career so he could stay in Readfield. "I was studying to be a teacher, but ended up in the plumbing business. If you have a trade, you can live wherever you want." When his parents retired in 1979, newlyweds John and Marjorie purchased the family house. John chuckles, "Luckily I found someone who wanted to live in the house I had grown up in. I like the house. I like being in town; I'm kind of a rooted person." Has John lived his entire life on Thundercastle Road? In true Maine fashion, he says, "Not yet."

It is easy to see why John wanted to stay in his childhood home. A 60-acre hardwood-conifer forest, including a stand of pines his parents planted in the early 1960's, surrounds the house. This was John and his brother Henry's playground. "We would go sledding with neighborhood kids, take make-believe walks in the woods, or make mud pies." The woods were also a chance for independence. "I'd put on my snowshoes and walk the land behind the house in the awkward years before I passed my driving test."

Over the years, the Tyler family considered a number of land management options. In the 1980's, a friend suggested selectively harvesting parts of it. Later, an out-of-town logger proposed a timber harvest. The results of the harvest were not what the Tylers expected. "The logger really didn't do us any favors, and we learned our lesson. We knew the land would recover, but not if it was subdivided." The family decided together to grant a conservation easement to the Kennebec Land Trust. "We knew it was the right thing to do."

In the trail log of the Tyler Conservation Area, visitors show appreciation for the woods and trails with messages like "beautiful forest" and "great walk." One enthusiastic visitor from Mexico wrote "Ay, caramba!" Messages like these make the donation rewarding for the Tylers, who have found working with KLT to benefit both their family and

John and Marjorie Tyler
(Jane Davis: 2009)

community. "How many people have a house surrounded by a land trust?" says John.

The brothers see the donation as a reflection of their parents' values. "Henry and I are finding out that our parents were behind-the-scenes people. They would support community projects and avoid recognition." By naming the conservation area after their parents, John and Henry honor them for their contributions to the community. "The land was meant to be a gift to the people of Readfield. We know it will be well-managed by and for future generations."

Good forestry is a long-term endeavor. For families that want to manage their land in a thoughtful, careful way, a conservation easement can help by assuring them that their efforts will be carried on by future generations.

— Morten Moesswilde, District Forester, Maine Forest Service

Tyler Woods *(Jym St. Pierre)*

VAUGHAN WOODS
CONSERVATION EASEMENT, HALLOWELL

LAND DONORS: GEORGE AND DIANA GIBSON
OWNED BY: VAUGHAN HOMESTEAD FOUNDATION

Vaughan Woods
(Jym St. Pierre)

Vaughan Woods in Hallowell offers a glimpse of American history in a landscape that is celebrated for its natural beauty. An average of 150 people a day visit this scenic, historic conservation property. Hallowell residents walk in the woods in every season, and many return with new generations of hikers who fall in love with its majestic trees, picturesque stone bridges, and carriage trails.

In 1628, King James I of England conveyed a large land grant that included the woods to the Plymouth Colony. The Colony in turn sold the land to the "Proprietors of the Kennebec Purchase" in 1661, but frequent wars between settlers and Native Americans prevented it from being occupied until after the Peace of Paris ended the French & Indian War in 1763. Benjamin Hallowell, a Boston merchant (Maine then being a part of Massachusetts) and Kennebec Proprietor for whom the city of Hallowell is named, took possession of Settler's Lot #22.

The property's story continued when Benjamin deeded the land to his son, Briggs Hallowell. Meanwhile, Benjamin's daughter, Sarah Hallowell, married Samuel Vaughan of London, England. Under English law, women could not inherit property. Thus, when Briggs died, the property passed not to his wife, but to Briggs' brother-in-law, Samuel Vaughan.

Samuel, in turn, left the land to his own son, Benjamin Vaughan, a former member of Parliament. Just before the turn of the century, his brother Charles built a house for him, which still stands today. In 1797, Benjamin moved in. A voracious reader, his library held the second-largest book collection in New England, after Harvard University.

Over the decades, the family developed sections of the property, and between 1890 and 1930, they constructed a network of trails in the woods. The property remained under shared family ownership until 1973. George and Diana Vaughan Gibson inherited a portion, and purchased the remaining shares from other family members. The Gibsons' three children, George, Ellen, and David, spent summers at the Homestead with their grandmother, and grew to appreciate its history. Few people came to the woods then, and the Gibsons remember those summers as a retreat for adventures and discovery.

David recalls that his parents had a real "sense of responsibility and stewardship. Preserving the land was something they always wanted."

Diana and
George Gibson
(Contributed)

Understanding the historical and ecological value of the woods, the Gibsons decided they should be conserved. In 1990, they granted a conservation easement on 152 acres of the original Vaughan Homestead to the Kennebec Land Trust.

Today, as the public wanders the Vaughan trails, they can see vivid reminders of the past. The Page and Stickney Dam, built in 1871, contains Cascade Pond, the granite quarry which supplied stone for the Homestead's foundation. Several stone and concrete arched bridges connect the trails. An old-growth white pine stand was declared a Special Natural Area by the State of Maine in 1983.

At the Vaughan Homestead, history, architecture, landscape, and nature converge to create one of the most treasured places of the Kennebec Valley.

— Earle Shettleworth, Jr., Maine State Historian

The Vaughan Homestead Foundation monitors and maintains the trails with help from local volunteers and the KLT. In addition, the Foundation works with the Maine Conservation Corps and the Trust on challenging trail projects. The Vaughan Woods has become one of the most beloved places in Hallowell. David says, "We are all blessed to know how much these woods mean as a place of recreation, education, respite, and spiritual retreat to so many people in the community. This could not have been possible without a strong partnership with KLT."

Vaughan Homestead *(Norm Rodrigue)*

Anne Warren, William Manning Vaughan, and daughter-in-law, Anna H. Vaughan
(Contributed, circa 1890)

WEBBER-ROGERS FARMSTEAD CONSERVATION AREA
CONSERVATION EASEMENT, LITCHFIELD

LAND DONORS: GEORGE AND JUDY ROGERS

Webber-Rogers Farmstead
(Sarah Fuller)

Every fall George Rogers walks, saw in hand, into the World War I vintage orchard where his father and grandfather tended to 1,000 apple trees. George cuts and splits five cords of wood to last through the winter. That's just one of the many farm chores.

George and his wife, Judy, also tend two gardens and grow vegetables that they store for the winter. George bush-hogs 15 acres of pasture and trims between rows of grapevines in the property's small vineyard. Then, of course, there is constant mending of fences and trails. It is the work all farmers and landowners do to maintain equilibrium between their spheres of domesticity and the forces of weather, decay, and persistent plant growth.

The Rogers and Webbers (George's mother's family) came to the Upper Pleasant Pond area in the late 1700's. After 32 years spent teaching in the Boston area, George and Judy returned to live full-time on the farm in 1997. They are combining retirement with new careers as small-scale farmers. However, George won't call the homestead a working farm.

"It hasn't been an active farm since the 1930's... ever since lightning hit the barn and it burned down." He grins and points to the short lightning rods perched atop the two-story home that sits on the old barn's foundation. "We're better prepared now."

All 117 acres of the Rogers' property are under conservation easement. 15 acres of hayfields are mowed by a neighboring dairy farmer. "If you leave those fields for a few years, forget it," argues George. "The next year it will have bushes three-feet tall." The trees on the rest of the Rogers' property are proof of George's warning. A dense, mixed-age forest covers the eastern half of the property, including several acres of former pasture.

The public has access to a mile and a half of hiking trails that wind through the forest and follow the wooded shoreline of Upper Pleasant Pond. The Rogers' two children, both competitive swimmers, grew up racing each other from the shoreline to the far side of the pond and back. Judy remembers that it was easier for her parents-in-law to go swimming. She jokes, "They didn't have to walk through a forest to get to the pond."

George and Judy's efforts to balance open farmland and forest have community benefits. The fields provide a surplus of hay for the neighboring farmer and a much-loved sledding hill in the winter.

For George and Judy, preserving the property with an easement has "value that exceeds any monetary consideration." Like many small land owners, they were worried that "the family land would be sold and developed." Active on town committees, both are concerned about the future of Litchfield, which is one of the fastest-growing towns in Kennebec County. "Once a farming community, Litchfield now has but a handful of active farms left."

The Rogers are grateful that they were able to consider a number of conservation options for their land. They believe their easement presents the best balance between preservation and growth. It will keep the land undeveloped, beautiful, yet open to agricultural use. The easement assures access for their family. They hope "future generations of the family will love and enjoy the land, too."

A simple equation: (George and Judy Rogers + 117 beautiful acres in Litchfield + trails + birds + woods + fields + waters) x (love of the land + concern for future generations) + The Kennebec Land Trust = Land conservation at its finest.

— Howard Lake,
   KLT Founding Board Member,

Judy and George Rogers
(Jane Davis: 2009)

Sledding at Webber-Rogers
(Jane Davis)

At present, KLT has the ongoing good fortune to have been offered ownership and conservation easements for several new properties, each of which closely matches our mission of preserving special lands that are representative of our area. These are properties which have outstanding natural features, wonderful plant and animal habitats, and offer, in some cases, additional public recreational opportunities or the preservation of traditional working landscapes. Many offer a fabulous combination of these valuable features!

We continue to be grateful to you, our generous supporters and donors, for offering these properties. Thank you for your generosity and thank you on behalf of the future generations who will look back at this work and say, "What a good idea!"

—*Cheryl Harrington,*
  President, KLT August 2009 – August 2011

Oak at Vaughan Woods *(Jym St. Pierre)*

Elvin Farm Walk *(Karen Simpson)*

Bog Pond *(Jym St. Pierre)*

(Karen Simpson)

CLEMEDOW FARM
MONMOUTH

MEADOW BROOK FARM
FAYETTE

CLEMEDOW FARM OWNER: JEREMIAH SMITH
MEADOW BROOK FARM OWNERS: BERNDT AND ELAINE GRAF

Smith Farm *(Jane Davis)*

Jerry Smith's great-grandfather and grandfather purchased Clemedow Farm in 1911. "When I was growing up in Monmouth, there were a lot of farms," he remembers. "At first we grew mostly apples, but sometime in the 1930's a bad freeze killed most of the apple trees. That looked like a good time to switch to dairy!"

Clemedow sells milk to Oakhurst Dairy, a Maine company that buys from small farms. "We have about 100 milkers and about 80 young cows." The first milking session goes from 3:30 a.m. until about 7:00. Jerry is back at 2:00 in the afternoon for round two. He and the farm's other full-time employee milk the cows "twice a day, 365 days a year. It's hard work, but it's what I want to do."

He feeds his cows only grass. "It's basically a grass farm, which means there's very little erosion. In return the cows make organic fertilizer. It's a good cycle."

Elaine and Berndt Graf started their Fayette dairy farm, Meadow Brook, in 1983. Berndt comes from a long line of farmers, and although he trained as a structural designer, farming was the only thing he ever wanted to do. Elaine's Maine roots go back to the 1960's when her father, Standish Bachman, was the Economic Development Commissioner for then Governor Reed.

Like Jerry, Berndt and Elaine believe that rural lands should be protected for the next generation. Their 245-acre organic dairy farm consists of 30 milking Jerseys plus young stock. They have a small fiber business from eight Romney/Finn sheep and two angora goats. Open land is devoted to pasture, though hay comes from distant fields they do not own.

In March, 2010, the Grafs acted on a long-held vision and purchased 90 acres that were contiguous to their current farm. They plan to return 65 acres to hay production; the eventual savings in time, fuel, and wear on equipment would allow them to expand into a small cheese and maple sugar business. With this purchase, the Grafs will not only be more self-sufficient, they will own more land than was part of their farm at the time of Fayette's settlement. "Having witnessed unplanned development of the wonderful rural places we grew up in, we have a great desire to do what we can to protect farmland."

The Grafs and Jerry Smith want to provide for recreational access to their properties. They see great value in the large wetlands that provide excellent habitat for birds, mammals, amphibians, and other wildlife on their farms. Jerry Smith is developing a plan whereby he will sell a conservation easement on 280 acres, enjoy a well-earned retirement, and help a new farmer get acquainted with the farm. The Grafs look to conserve 230 acres of their enlarged property and diversify their business. The properties will be monitored to ensure that they remain in agriculture, an ideal outcome for small Maine farmers who want to do what is best for the land.

Jeremiah Smith
(Jane Davis: 2009)

Elaine and Berndt Graf
(Contributed)

KLT Abigail Holman Agricultural Education Program
(Karen Simpson)

Land conservation projects involving working landscapes — both farms and woodlots — are particularly challenging and immensely rewarding. These projects not only protect special places — they also provide for people's livelihoods, preserve a rural way of life, and support sustainable local economies.

— Jerry Bley, Creative Conservation

45

CELEBRATING OUR ROOTS

We end with a tribute to our beginning. In August of 1988, a group of citizens assembled in Readfield to give birth to the Kennebec Land Trust as one of the first inland land trusts in Maine. Inspired by the vision of Jym St. Pierre and Howard Lake, those present embarked on a bold experiment to try to preserve (in their words) "a livable countryside to pass down to future generations." Just two years later, Diana and George Gibson expressed their faith in the budding land trust by donating a conservation easement, forever preserving the cherished Vaughan Woods in Hallowell.

Today, KLT's protected lands encompass nearly 3,700 acres covering some 50 properties in communities throughout the Kennebec River and Lakes region. KLT's work is supported by more than 700 members, a legion of dedicated land stewards and volunteers, an activist board of directors and advisory board, and a widely respected executive director. Through all their efforts, KLT has become the leading instrument of land conservation in our region.

None of this, from the original vision to the present day, has been the product of fortunate happenstance; all has required faith, perseverance, generosity, and hard work. KLT's supporters have donated their land, time, and money toward achieving that early vision of "preserving a livable countryside." While the work continues, we celebrate a grand beginning, with more wonders to unfold in the decades ahead.

— *Jeff Pidot, KLT Advisory Board; President, August 1997 - August 1999.*

Mount Pisgah (Jym St. Pierre)

Parker Pond Headland (Jym St. Pierre)

LAND CONSERVATION ORGANIZATIONS AND AGENCIES

Maine's Local and Regional Land Trusts

Local and regional land trusts play an essential role in Maine's conservation community. Trusts own land, hold and monitor conservation easements, help landowners develop conservation plans, educate people about the value of open space, and raise funds to purchase threatened properties. The total acreage held by land trusts nationwide (not counting lands transferred to state or federal agencies) now exceeds one million acres. Most of Maine's local land trusts are staffed by volunteers, although a growing number have paid staff.

Kennebec Land Trust

PO Box 261
134 Main Street
Winthrop, Maine 04364
207-377-2848 *www.tklt.org*

Kennebec Land Trust focuses on protecting the important natural areas and working landscapes of the Kennebec River and Lakes region of Kennebec County. As a regional land trust, we work cooperatively with landowners in a twenty-two-town area centered around the state capital. Currently we own 2,539 acres and hold conservation easements on 1,026 acres. These conservation lands feature twenty miles of trails and eight miles of shoreline.

Maine Land Trust Network c/o Maine Coast Heritage Trust (MCHT)

1 Bowdoin Mill Island, Suite 201,
Topsham, ME 04086
(207) 729-7366 *www.mltn.org*

The **MLTN**, a program of (**MCHT**), is a communications and coordination service provided by Maine Coast Heritage Trust to land conservation organizations throughout the state. To locate a local land trust or for further information, contact:

Land Trust Alliance (LTA)

1331 H St. NW, Suite 400
Washington, DC 20005-4734
202-638-4725 *www.lta.org*

The **LTA** promotes voluntary land conservation and strengthens the land trust movement by providing the leadership, information and resources that land trusts need to conserve land for the benefit of communities and natural systems.

Maine Coast Heritage Trust (MCHT)

1 Main Street, Suite 201
Topsham, ME 04086
207-729-7366 *www.mcht.org*

MCHT protects coastal and other lands of scenic, ecological, recreational and cultural significance. The Trust provides free conservation services to landowners, government agencies, local land trusts and communities statewide.

FORESTLAND CONSERVATION

Kennebec Woodland Partnership (KWP): KWP is a forestland conservation initiative that promotes private and public land stewardship and conservation in Kennebec County. The Partnership's goal is to provide a wide range of tools and strategies to help landowners make informed decisions about their woodlands. Rather than a one-size-fits-all solution, the Partnership supports a range of actions and commitments that lead toward keeping forest as forest in Kennebec County. The Partnership was formed out of common interests and an awareness that Kennebec County's local economy, wood products markets, recreational opportunities, water quality, wildlife habitat, and quality of life all depend largely on approximately 388,000 acres of woodland. The Kennebec Woodland Partnership aims to work with a broad network of woodland owners, local businesses, towns, cities, timber harvesters, foresters, and biologists, with support from local conservation groups, state agencies, and non-profit organizations. The Partnership has seven lead partners:

LEAD CONTACT

Maine Forest Service	Kennebec Land Trust	Kennebec County Soil and Water Conservation District	Small Woodland Owners Association of Maine	Trust to Conserve Northeast Forestlands	Forest Society of Maine	Maine Forest Products Council
Morten Moesswilde District Forester 2870 North Belfast Avenue Augusta, Maine 04330 (207)441-2895 *www.maine.gov*	PO Box 261 134 Main Street Winthrop, Maine 04364 207-377-2848 *www.tklt.org*	Kennebec Soil & Water Conservation District 21 Enterprise Dr., Suite #1 Augusta, ME 04330 (207)622-7847 x3 *www.kcswcd.org*	153 Hospital Street P. O. Box 836Augusta, ME 04332-0836 (207)626-0005 *www.swoam.org*	41 Pineland Drive Suite 201A New Gloucester, ME 04260 (207) 688-8195 *www.tcnef.org*	115 Franklin St. 3rd Floor Bangor, ME 04401 (207)945-9200 *www.fsmaine.org*	535 Civic Center Drive Augusta, ME 04330 (207)622-9288 *www.maineforest.org*

Wildlands and Woodlands: Harvard Forest, 324 North Main Street, Petersham, MA 01366. *http://www.wildlandsandwoodlands.org*
Wildlands and Woodlands is a vision for the future that calls for the conservation of at least 70 percent of the New England region in forestland. Wildlands and Woodlands attempts to balance the interests of forest management and forest preservation in order to protect the forest base that supports human livelihood and biodiversity in New England.

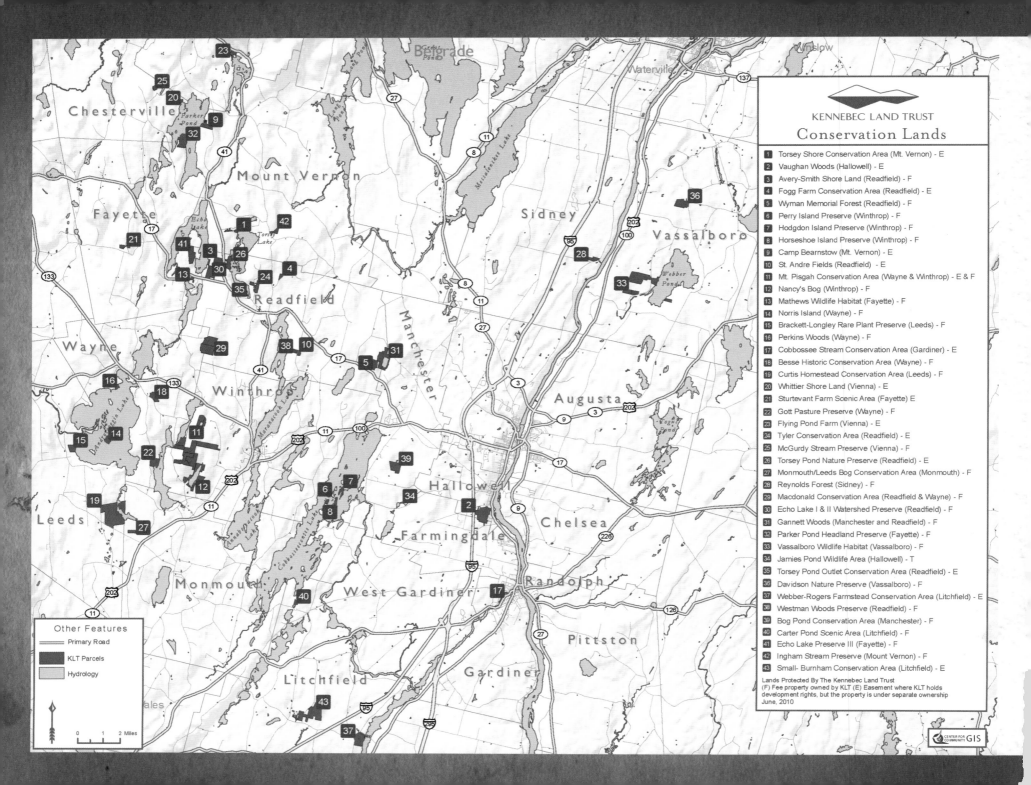

KENNEBEC LAND TRUST
Conservation Lands

1. Torsey Shore Conservation Area (Mt. Vernon) - E
2. Vaughan Woods (Hallowell) - E
3. Avery-Smith Shore Land (Readfield) - F
4. Fogg Farm Conservation Area (Readfield) - E
5. Wyman Memorial Forest (Readfield) - F
6. Perry Island Preserve (Winthrop) - F
7. Hodgdon Island Preserve (Winthrop) - F
8. Horseshoe Island Preserve (Winthrop) - F
9. Camp Bearnstow (Mt. Vernon) - E
10. St. Andre Fields (Readfield) - E
11. Mt. Pisgah Conservation Area (Wayne & Winthrop) - E & F
12. Nancy's Bog (Winthrop) - F
13. Mathews Wildlife Habitat (Fayette) - F
14. Norris Island (Wayne) - F
15. Brackett-Longley Rare Plant Preserve (Leeds) - F
16. Perkins Woods (Wayne) - F
17. Cobbossee Stream Conservation Area (Gardiner) - E
18. Besse Historic Conservation Area (Wayne) - F
19. Curtis Homestead Conservation Area (Leeds) - F
20. Whittier Shore Land (Vienna) - E
21. Sturtevant Farm Scenic Area (Fayette) E
22. Gott Pasture Preserve (Wayne) - F
23. Flying Pond Farm (Vienna) - E
24. Tyler Conservation Area (Readfield) - E
25. McGurdy Stream Preserve (Vienna) - F
26. Torsey Pond Nature Preserve (Readfield) - E
27. Monmouth/Leeds Bog Conservation Area (Monmouth) - F
28. Reynolds Forest (Sidney) - F
29. Macdonald Conservation Area (Readfield & Wayne) - F
30. Echo Lake I & II Watershed Preserve (Readfield) - F
31. Gannett Woods (Manchester and Readfield) - F
32. Parker Pond Headland Preserve (Fayette) - F
33. Vassalboro Wildlife Habitat (Vassalboro) - F
34. Jamies Pond Wildlife Area (Hallowell) - T
35. Torsey Pond Outlet Conservation Area (Readfield) - E
36. Davidson Nature Preserve (Vassalboro) - F
37. Webber-Rogers Farmstead Conservation Area (Litchfield) - E
38. Westman Woods Preserve (Readfield) - F
39. Bog Pond Conservation Area (Manchester) - F
40. Carter Pond Scenic Area (Litchfield) - F
41. Echo Lake Preserve III (Fayette) - F
42. Ingham Stream Preserve (Mount Vernon) - F
43. Small- Burnham Conservation Area (Litchfield) - E

Lands Protected By The Kennebec Land Trust
(F) Fee property owned by KLT (E) Easement where KLT holds
development rights, but the property is under separate ownership
June, 2010

Other Features
— Primary Road
▬ KLT Parcels
▨ Hydrology

0   1   2 Miles

CENTER FOR COMMUNITY GIS